KT-452-086

Contents

Introduction

Welcome to this School Induction Pack

This pack will:

- highlight the value of Adults Supporting Learning (ASL) who assist in physical education (PE) and school sport
- provide guidance and offer support material for teachers, head teachers and governors when inducting ASL into the school environment and ethos
- remind schools that they have a responsibility to both young people and ASL
- assist schools in increasing the effectiveness of ASL contribution to physical education and school sport
- remind schools that it is their responsibility to provide support and guidance for the ASL in the wider educational context
- support teachers working with ASL
- help new ASL understand and carry out their roles in the education process
- assist teachers in encouraging ASL to move forward and progress
- provide information that can support the development of ASL.

Pages containing the Photocopy symbol in the top right-hand corner may be photocopied without permission, for distribution to teachers and ASL. All other pages contain copyright material, and permission to reproduce them must be sought from **Coachwise Ltd**[1].

Who are Adults Supporting Learning?

ASL are those people who do not hold a recognised teaching qualification (although they may hold other relevant qualifications) but, with the permission of the head teacher and governors, contribute to the delivery of physical education and school sport in a variety of ways. The list of ASL commonly includes:

- local authority sports development officers (SDOs)
- national governing body (NGB) coaches and development officers
- community sports coaches
- other coaches, instructors, parents and helpers
- community sports leaders
- further education (FE)/higher education (HE) college students
- trainees who are undergoing initial teacher-training programmes.

There are many types of ASL who work in schools, and it is important that the head teachers differentiate the support and supervision they require. It is the responsibility of the head teacher to determine whether the ASL have the appropriate skills, and to ensure that they meet clear safeguarding and protecting children criteria (see *Workforce Reform – Essential Safe Practice in Physical Education and School Sport*, baalpe 2005).

There are two types of ASL:

- **Stage One ASL** have little or no experience or expertise in physical education or school sport. They should always work directly alongside a designated teacher, even if they are experienced.
- **Stage Two ASL** have a certain level of technical knowledge about their sport, acquired through a coaching qualification or equivalent. They should initially work alongside a designated teacher, but may be allowed to work at distance when they are able to demonstrate an appropriate level of expertise, knowledge of safety issues and a positive attitude towards pupils.

1 See page 35 for contact details.

ASL:

- **always** work under the direction of a designated teacher(s)
- **often** work alongside and assist teachers
- **may** work at distance from teachers, providing:
  - they have the appropriate status, expertise and knowledge of the pupils
  - the results of a risk assessment support this
  - there is appropriate insurance in place (see footnote 1 on page 4)
- are used to:
  - support the delivery of the curriculum in lesson time
  - develop out-of-school-hours clubs and teams on the school site
  - deliver off-site activities, providing they have the competence and confidence to do so.

How ASL are involved will depend on the:

- employer's (LA/governors/trustees) policy on the use of ASL
- ASL level of expertise, qualifications and availability.

What Support is Available?

Support should be provided at two levels and the following resources are available:

- **Stage One**: This *School Induction Pack* will help the school *induct* ASL into the working environment and ethos of the school.
- **Stage Two**: Following on from the *School Induction Pack*, more experienced ASL can attend a Physical Education Awareness Course for ASL[1] to gain a greater insight into the subject. Among other aspects, it focuses on topics such as safeguarding and protecting children, differentiation, the National Curriculum, teaching and learning, and wider government strategies such as *Every Child Matters*.

Question: Who should use the ASL School Induction Pack?

Answer: This pack should be used by any school that has ASL (see page 1 for definition) working in lessons or out-of-school-hours activities in physical education and school sport. The correct support and management of ASL in schools will ensure that the school, the young people and the ASL will mutually benefit from the experience.

Question: Why should you use the ASL School Induction Pack?

Answer: This pack gives detailed information on how to provide a professional induction for any ASL working in schools. Working through the pack with the ASL, the school will be able to support the ASL to become more familiar with the protocol and ethos of their school and will, therefore, be more effective in their role. Teachers are provided with a step-by-step manual to guide themselves and ASL through practicalities, such as kit policy, and more sensitive issues, such as child protection. ASL will be encouraged to keep a portfolio that will demonstrate their competencies and experiences in the physical education and school sport environment. Once a desired level of experience and competence has been gained, ASL can then access the second level of support through the Physical Education Awareness Course for ASL.

1 See page 16 for further details.

Introduction

> ### Question: What does the Physical Education Awareness Course for ASL involve?
>
> **Answer:** This course is designed for ASL who wish to extend their knowledge of physical education and school sport. During the course, ASL will explore various educational themes, such as differentiation and teaching/learning strategies. A brief summary of the National Curriculum will be provided, as well as an introduction to planning sessions. This information, combined with a thorough induction programme, should ensure that ASL have sufficient educational knowledge and experience to become much more than just an extra pair of hands.
>
> ### Question: If you are interested, what do you do next?
>
> **Answer:** For further information about the Physical Education Awareness Course for ASL, please contact afPE[1] or log on to www.sportscoachuk.org
>
> For further career advice and support, please contact the afPE National College for Continuing Professional Development at www.afpe.org.uk

Working with ASL

ASL can considerably enhance the delivery of the physical education curriculum, extended schools programmes and out-of-school-hours learning activities.

What can ASL offer you?

- Expertise in specific activities
- Role models
- Enthusiasm
- Help within the curriculum
- Flexibility
- Help with out-of-school-hours learning activities and extended schools programmes
- Community links.

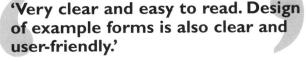

'Very clear and easy to read. Design of example forms is also clear and user-friendly.'

Jeanne Clatworthy, Worley Town School

What can you offer ASL?

- A valuable, enjoyable experience and an opportunity to contribute to the development of young people
- Opportunities to help deliver sporting activities
- Opportunities to extend their own learning
- Support for continuing professional development (CPD) opportunities
- Employment.

It is important to remember that the ASL should enjoy their time at your school. As a result, their commitment to the school and the programme will strengthen.

The correct support and management should always begin with a good induction programme, which includes direct delivery, safeguarding and protecting children, and basic awareness training.

1 See Appendix 6 for contact details.

Guidelines for Good Practice

Screening of ASL

Even though all ASL will work under the direction of a designated teacher(s), it is essential that, during recruitment, the school adopts a screening procedure. Screening is the process of checking the suitability of ASL, to ensure they have the relevant qualifications, knowledge, skills, attitudes, behaviour and experience to work with young people. These checks should include:

- enhanced Criminal Records Bureau disclosure certification, in line with School Staffing (Amendment) Regulations 2006
- NGB qualification validity
- appropriate insurance cover[1]
- experience/training that is age-related and relevant to working with young people (eg a recognised child protection basic awareness workshop)
- agreement to NGB/sports coach UK's *Code of Practice for Sports Coaches*
- an up-to-date first-aid qualification (desirable)
- up-to-date references, relating to the suitability of the ASL for this role and to him/her working with children
- specific expertise, if required (eg working with people with special needs, particular age groups, females).

For details of how to apply for disclosure certification, see Appendix 1.

1 Coaches as school support staff will be covered by the school's insurance policy. The school should check that agency coaches have insurance cover equivalent to that of the school. Self-employed coaches can take out afPE ASL insurance, which enables them to work alone. Without any of these, ASL with NGB insurance would be limited to working alongside a teacher. The school, agency or afPE insurance would supersede any NGB insurance and allow the ASL to work alone.

Core Principles in Children's Physical Education and School Sport

Outlined below are the core principles of Long-term Athlete Development in children's physical education and school sport. Teachers and ASL should work through these carefully, explaining each point.

The key principles that characterise this LTAD model are:

- It takes approximately 10 years of extensive practice to excel in anything; if potential is to be realised, there are no shortcuts.

- The nature of the growing child and the early stages of development must be a central consideration when planning and implementing coaching programmes.

- Differences in the nature of sports, whether they require young people to specialise in them at an early age or later, are key to determining training and competition programmes.

- The fundamental skills and physical literacy, gained during a child's early sport experiences, in subsequent development, are vitally important.

- Windows of trainability that appear at different times during maturation should be paid particular attention. If these windows are fully appreciated and exploited, the training effect will be optimal and will significantly help true potential to be realised.

- Young athletes' competitive and training programmes should be reviewed. This might involve more innovative and creative thinking from coaches, as well as a restructuring of competitive experiences. Coaches are challenged to consider what they can do and what they can influence.

- Involving a whole range of significant other people such as parents, teachers, administrators, fixture secretaries and officials, in order to produce an integrated and progressive sport experience for young people, is necessary.

- Striving for system integration or pulling it all together for the athlete, in terms of sport experience in schools and clubs, coaching programmes, coach education, competitive structures and appropriate support systems, is a key requirement.

- Committing to continuous improvement is important. The LTAD model should reflect good coaching practice in terms of being constantly reviewed and improved in the light of research evidence and changing environments.

The LTAD principles given above have been reproduced from the sports coach UK resource *Coaching for Long-term Athlete Development*. For further information and to purchase a copy, please visit www.1st4sport.com, quoting B23709.

Guidelines for Good Practice

Every Child Matters

It is crucial that you encompass the five key outcomes of the *Every Child Matters Green Paper* (Crown, 2003) to ensure you are meeting the expectations of the government's five-year strategy. Listed below are these five outcomes and you should consider where physical education makes a contribution to achieving them for every child.

Every child has a right to:

be healthy

✓ physically healthy

✓ mentally and emotionally healthy

✓ sexually healthy

✓ have a healthy lifestyle

✓ choose not to take illegal drugs

stay safe

✓ safe from maltreatment, neglect, violence and sexual exploitation

✓ safe from accidental injury and death

✓ safe from bullying and discrimination

✓ safe from crime and antisocial behaviour, in and out of school

✓ have security, stability and be cared for

enjoy and achieve

✓ ready for school

✓ attend and enjoy school

✓ achieve stretching national education standards at primary school

✓ achieve personal and social development and enjoy recreation

✓ achieve stretching national educational standards at secondary school

make a positive contribution

✓ engage in decision making and support the community and the environment

✓ engage in law-abiding and positive behaviour, in and out of school

✓ develop positive relationships and choose not to bully or discriminate

✓ develop self-confidence and successfully deal with significant life changes and challenges

✓ develop enterprising behaviour

achieve economic well-being

✓ engage in further education, employment or training after leaving school

✓ be ready for employment

✓ live in a decent home and a sustainable community

✓ have access to transport and material goods

✓ live in a household free from low income.

Guidelines for Good Practice

Do's ✓ and Don'ts ✗

Here are some basic good-practice ideas to follow when working with ASL. Work through these, taking time to explain the rationale behind them.

Do...

- welcome ASL to the school
- offer appropriate information
- ensure that they are aware of and understand appropriate policies/procedures
- explain relevant policies (eg behaviour, health and safety, safeguarding and protecting children)
- ensure they know who they will be responsible to
- give them realistic/reasonable/responsible tasks matching their level of expertise and competence
- give them support and guidance
- include them in relevant decision making and risk assessments
- learn from the experience ASL may bring to the school
- expect young people to respect ASL
- encourage ASL to develop
- encourage ASL to keep a development portfolio.

Don't...

- take ASL for granted
- give them responsibility beyond their competence or level of confidence
- assume they are experts in physical education
- expect them to complete inappropriate school paperwork
- leave Stage One ASL alone in charge of an individual pupil or a group of young people
- leave Stage Two ASL alone in charge of an individual pupil or a group of young people without:
  - carrying out a thorough risk assessment
  - obtaining an enhanced level disclosure certificate
  - ensuring that their level of expertise, attitude towards pupils, and application of the school's standards and policies are appropriate[1]
  - agreeing a teaching programme
  - arranging to visit them regularly, to monitor their work.

The CPD that you offer your ASL should be as practical and work-related as possible.

---

1 For further information on recommended standards and competencies, visit the afPE website (www.afpe.org.uk).

Guidelines for Good Practice

Duty of Care

- Employers (local authorities [LAs], governors or trustees) are legally responsible for all aspects of health and safety. Schools benefiting from the contributions of ASL must ensure that they follow their employer's policy on the use of ASL.

- Teachers are always ultimately responsible for all aspects of pupil health, safety and learning. However, every adult has a duty to ensure the welfare, and health and safety of the young people with whom they work.

- It is your responsibility to work with, and manage, ASL to ensure that they work in a safe, effective manner, which totally assists the work of your school.

- ASL should initially work directly alongside a designated teacher(s). They should only work at distance from the teacher when they are able to demonstrate an appropriate level of expertise, knowledge and understanding of safety and child protection issues, and a positive attitude towards pupils.

- All out-of-school-hours activities should be carried out under the overall responsibility of a teacher, even though the teacher may not be involved in the activity session.

- You must assume that Stage One ASL have no experience or expertise in physical education or school sport, and should ensure that they always work directly alongside a designated teacher(s) during lessons, out-of-school-hours activities and educational visits. It may not be necessary to obtain disclosure certification for Stage One ASL if they will never be left alone with pupils. Check with your employer what level of disclosure, if any, is required.

- Stage Two ASL should initially work alongside a designated teacher(s). They may be allowed to work at distance from, but still managed by, the teacher, providing:
  - a thorough risk assessment has been carried out
  - an enhanced level disclosure certificate has been obtained
  - their level of expertise, attitude towards pupils, and application of the school's standards and policies are appropriate
  - a teaching programme has been agreed
  - arrangements have been made to visit them regularly to monitor their work.

Note: In certain circumstances, it may be decided that a Stage Two ASL needs to work alongside a designated teacher, even if he/she fulfils the above criteria.

> Further details on recommended standards and competencies relating to ASL can be found on the afPE website (www.afpe.org.uk).

Declaration

I agree to work within the requirements of the Children Acts 1989 and 2004[1] and to always ensure that the ASL is working under the direction of a teacher.

Signature of subject leader: _____ Date: _____

I agree to work within the requirements of the Children Acts 1989 and 2004 and to always work under the direction of a teacher.

Signature of ASL: _____ Date: _____

Please photocopy for each ASL involved. Both the ASL and the school will keep a copy.

---

1 Please contact your employer for more information on the Children Act and other related legislation and guidance.

Safeguarding and Protecting Children – Ensuring Safe Learning, Teaching and Coaching Practice

Physical education and school sport can have a very powerful influence on young people. The welfare of all young people should be fully understood and should guide how we work with and develop them.

Some of the ASL who enter your school may have had some safeguarding and protecting children awareness continuing professional development from one of a number of training providers, including sports coach UK, the NSPCC, afPE or their NGB. However, it should never be assumed that all people are aware of the issues surrounding child protection.

The guidance provided in Appendices 7 and 8 will help to ensure a baseline of awareness:

> - **Safe and Sound (2005)**
>   Childline, sports coach UK, Sport England, NSPCC
>   *(See Appendix 7 for a copy of the leaflet)*
>
> - **Code of Practice for Sports Coaches (2005)**
>   sports coach UK
>   *(See Appendix 8 for a copy of the leaflet)*

Please ensure that ASL are given the opportunity to read, adopt and abide by the philosophies and advice that these appendices provide.

Declaration

I have read the *Safe and Sound* leaflet (see Appendix 7).

Signature of ASL: _____ Date: _____

I have read and adopted the principles within the *Code of Practice for Sports Coaches* (see Appendix 8).

Signature of ASL: _____ Date: _____

> For further details on training opportunities in safeguarding and protecting children, please see 'Section 5: Moving On' later in this pack.

Please photocopy for each ASL involved. Both the ASL and the school will keep a copy.

Induction and Planning

Welcome to the School

The induction of an ASL into school involves awareness of the overarching philosophy that guides the policies and procedures within the school (eg the school mission statement, behaviour policy and the safeguarding and protecting of children).

The school will have a number of existing resources to help achieve this. The aim should be to make the ASL comfortable and confident with the information they receive. It is appreciated that there may be a vast amount of information for the ASL to take in and that this may take some time.

Recommended induction into the school

- Meeting the staff:
  - School
  - Physical education teachers/relevant class teachers
  - School Sport Coordinators (SSCos)
  - Partnership Development Manager (PDM)
  - Director of Specialism
  - Other ASL
  - Secretary, caretaker, etc
- Copy of school staff handbook
- Copies of policies:
  - School aims
  - School rules
  - Rewards and sanctions
  - Health and safety
  - Behaviour
  - Dress (ASL and pupil)
  - Language and vocabulary (ASL and pupil)
  - English as an additional language (EAL)
  - Equal opportunities
  - Fair play
  - Safeguarding and protecting children
- Procedures:
  - Risk management
  - Emergency contact details
  - Accident and emergency procedures
  - Supervision
  - Disciplinary procedures
  - Payment arrangements (if applicable).

An induction checklist is provided in Appendix 2. You may wish to provide the ASL with copies of any documentation relating to the areas of induction listed above, and in Appendix 2.

Induction and Planning

Information Relating to the Physical Education Session

The level of information and awareness required by the ASL will depend upon their experience and specific role. ASL who are leading sessions will require more information than those assisting.

Information required by all ASL:

- Facilities and equipment
- Changing arrangements
- A policy on attendance and punctuality of young people and ASL
- Routine procedures before, during and after the session
- A physical education policy (eg kit policy, a policy on wearing jewellery and a policy for non-participants).

Information for all ASL leading the session

- **The need for preparing schemes of work and individual session planning**

    A scheme of work sets out a plan for learning over a defined period of time, which incorporates the skills, knowledge and understanding (four aspects) to be delivered through the programmes of study in the National Curriculum. The plan ensures progression in learning and achievement, and the outcomes will support the assessment process at the end of the Key Stage.

    Each session is planned in detail from the scheme of work and subsequent sessions should be revised according to the amount of learning achieved each time.

    ASL should be aware of these principles of planning, so that they fully understand the expected outcomes of a scheme, of a session, and of individual practice. It is in the short-term detailed session planning that strategies must be identified, in order to meet individuals' learning needs.

    Reference: QCA schemes of work using core tasks and *Assessment for Learning in Physical Education* (baalpe, 2005).

    A sample session plan is provided in Appendix 3.

- **Baselining**

    ASL should be aware of a group's starting point. Baselining young people in the activity to ensure continuity is very important. All schemes of work and session plans should build on the learning that has gone before.

    This information should be available from school staff and from school documentation.

Induction and Planning

Effective planning for working with ASL

When utilising the expertise of ASL in curriculum and out-of-school-hours activities, the school should:

- insist that teachers manage the work of ASL at all times
- carry out a risk assessment which considers expertise, attitude, pupil behaviour, class management and control, and the overall health and safety of the class
- develop a procedure for shared planning of the session content
- set a clear role and outline the responsibilities of the ASL
- require clear, regular communication between the teacher and ASL, to ensure that essential information is shared (eg the numbers in the group, any relevant medical information, pupils experiencing situations such as bereavement/divorce)
- determine a system for clearly identifying the role and responsibilities that each adult is taking
- ensure consistency in its procedures when ASL work with a number of teachers, so that the pupils experience a secure working environment
- provide CPD for ASL (eg Physical Education Awareness Course for ASL) in the content, requirements and delivery of the National Curriculum
- emphasise the need to educate the child, rather than teach the activity
- ensure that ASL understand and can apply differentiated equipment, tasks and levels of support to the needs of individuals, as appropriate
- encourage teachers and ASL to conduct shared pre-session risk assessments of the environment and context of the session
- develop effective pupil-led warm-up/session preparation, which is regularly monitored to check effectiveness, safety and understanding
- ensure that ASL understand and can apply the school's accident and post-accident procedures
- ensure that ASL who are supporting a teacher have some understanding of the context of a session within the scheme of work
- ensure that ASL leading the session fully understand the context of the session within the scheme of work.

This should ultimately lead to an effective team approach to teaching and learning.

'Our most successful partnerships of teachers and ASL have resulted in the significant raising of standards'

Janet Thorpe, Kirklees Local Authority

Monitoring, Evaluating and Reviewing

School self-review is important for the following reasons:

- It helps you to make an informed view of the performance and quality of Physical Education and School Sport (PESS) in your school.
- It ensures effective monitoring and evaluation processes are in place.
- It highlights strengths and celebrates successes.
- It identifies areas where further development is needed and highlights significant challenges and priorities.
- It provides a basis for you to set out the direction PESS is taking.
- It provides evidence to explain how PESS is meeting challenges.
- It shows that you are self-critical, reflective and are planning for improvement, through clear strategic thinking.
- It identifies staff CPD needs.
- It provides a check on health and safety procedures.
- It shows you are committed to raising standards, not only for the young people in your school, but also for all staff working with them.

Managing and supporting ASL is a continuous process and does not stop at the end of the induction programme. Although Stage One ASL will always work under the direct supervision of a teacher, it is good practice to build in monitoring and evaluation procedures, and self-evaluation processes. This can be of mutual benefit to the school, the ASL and the young people.

Stage Two ASL may work at some distance from a teacher and it is, therefore, necessary that regular monitoring and evaluation procedures are in place. This should ensure an effective self-evaluation process is in place, and will contribute to high-quality PESS outcomes for all young people.

Benefits for ASL

- Provides continuous support throughout their time at the school.
- Identifies development opportunities.
- Improves them as a practitioner.

'**Self-review enables you to know what you are achieving and what you need to do to improve. It also enables you to celebrate success from a position of strength, based on rigorous qualitative and quantitative evidence.**'

Peter Whitlam

Monitoring, Evaluating and Reviewing

Benefits for Young People

*   Reap the rewards of a high standard of delivery.
*   Feel involved in the process of evaluation.

There are a number of ways to monitor and evaluate activities. For all ASL, regular observation by the teacher should be a minimum requirement. Below are some suggestions that may also be appropriate at a later stage of development:

*   Keeping a delivery log
*   Evaluation forms
*   Appraisal of ASL
*   Accurate feedback from the teacher
*   Relevant CPD opportunities
*   Self-evaluation and reflection
*   Peer evaluation
*   Consultation and feedback from children and young people
*   Coaching and mentoring.

Reference: *A Guide to Self-review in Physical Education* (baalpe, 2006)

A sample delivery log is provided in Appendix 4. This will help ASL to document their own progress in a particular session, or series of sessions.

Sample feedback and evaluation forms are provided in Appendix 5. These will help ASL and teachers/mentors to obtain/provide feedback on both the ASL development and the induction process.

In addition, all of the above documents could be used as the basis for any appraisals involving ASL.

'The contribution of ASL in curriculum physical education will make a significant impact in raising standards.'

Eileen Marchant, Policy Adviser, afPE

Moving On

In Section 4, one of the main benefits mentioned is the identification of CPD needs. These needs can be identified both by the ASL and the teacher.

In the previous section, it is also suggested that ASL keep a delivery log. This process can contribute to the compilation of a development portfolio. This portfolio will provide evidence of experience and CPD opportunities that the ASL has undertaken, and demonstrate improved knowledge and understanding.

The direction of development will depend on the individual's baseline. The content of development will depend on the individual's aspirations.

Development Opportunities

Unqualified Helper (Stage One)

> **Remember:** All **Stage One ASL** should work directly alongside a designated teacher, even if they are experienced.

- A **Stage One ASL** may wish to remain at this level, without taking on any continuing professional development opportunities. However, it would be good practice to encourage gaining a first-aid qualification.
- An aspiring **Stage One ASL** may have enjoyed the experience so far and wish to progress further. If this is the case, there are a number of options available, including:
  - NGB Leader Awards
  - NGB Level One Coaching Awards
  - the sports coach UK workshops 'How to Coach Children in Sport' and 'Safeguarding and Protecting Children'
  - the EduCare Child Protection Awareness resource
  - a Community Sports Leaders Award
  - first-aid qualifications
  - the Physical Education Awareness Course.

NB: This is not a definitive list.

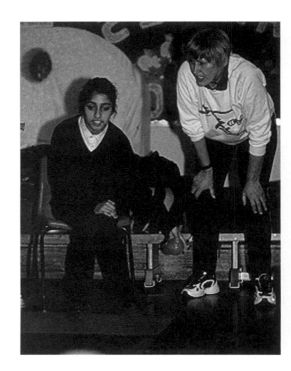

'**We are a new school who want to develop our use of ASL – this pack will give us a clear structure.**'

Tony Nelson, Shenley Brook End School

Moving On

Qualified Coach (Stage Two)

Remember: Stage Two ASL may work alongside, or at distance from, teachers.

*   A **Stage Two ASL** will have a certain level of technical knowledge about the sport, acquired through a coaching qualification. The level of knowledge will depend on the level of qualification the ASL has undertaken. This level of knowledge will be further enhanced by the ASL's level of experience.

*   The coaches can bring expertise in specific activities – however, they will benefit from CPD in physical education and generic educational principles.

*   This *School Induction Pack* is the first step in raising ASL awareness of physical education. To complement it, a Physical Education Awareness Course for ASL has been developed, to help qualified coaches working in the school environment fully understand their role in enhancing physical education.

*   It is strongly advised that all ASL operating as qualified coaches undertake the Physical Education Awareness Course before starting to lead sessions at distance from a teacher.

*   Schools will be able to verify a coach's attendance of the Physical Education Awareness Course, by asking to inspect his/her certificate of attendance, which will be awarded to all course participants. Schools will be able to check the authenticity of the certificate by looking for evidence of validation (a coloured sticker and the tutor's signature).

*   **Stage Two ASL** should be encouraged to keep a development portfolio. **Stage One ASL** can also keep a development portfolio if they wish to do so.

*   For more information about the Physical Education Awareness Course for ASL, please contact afPE[1], your LA or check out the sports coach UK website (www.sportscoachuk.org).

*   Other development opportunities include:
    *   the next level of NGB qualification
    *   NGB workshops
    *   sports coach UK workshops, including 'Safeguarding and Protecting Children', 'Coaching Children and Young People' and 'Equity in Your Coaching'
    *   FE/HE accredited education courses.

Teacher

*   Working alongside qualified coaches may give teachers an indication of some continuing professional development needs, which may include:
    *   NGB qualifications
    *   NGB workshops
    *   sports coach UK workshops, including 'Safeguarding and Protecting Children'
    *   LEA/national physical education CPD courses
    *   higher education institute-accredited (HEI) CPD.

There are a number of professional development providers who offer a variety of courses, workshops and resources. Their contact details can be found in Appendix 6.

---

1 See Appendix 6 for contact details.

Moving On

Further Information

Coaching for Teachers for the development of ASL

As part of the National Physical Education and School Sport Professional Development Programme, launched by the Department for Education and Skills (DfES) in 2003, *Coaching for Teachers* provides CPD opportunities for teachers and ASL who contribute to physical education and school sport.

The programme, delivered through the NGBs of sport and other training agencies, and supported by the DfES and coordinated by sports coach UK, aims to support teachers and ASL in improving their teaching and coaching skills, updating their sport-specific knowledge and obtaining relevant governing body qualifications.

For further information, please visit www.sportscoachuk.org

Alternatively, contact:

sports coach UK
114 Cardigan Road
Headingley
Leeds LS6 3BJ
Tel: 0113-274 4802
Fax: 0113-275 5019
Email: coaching@sportscoachuk.org

'I was inspired after attending the sports coach UK 'Introduction to FUNdamentals' workshop, recognising that the information delivered and the opportunities for exploring the taught concepts would be of great benefit to my local primary school teachers.'

Duncan Tucker, Partnership Development Manager for the South Northamptonshire School Sports Partnership

Summary

Working through this pack should have:

- highlighted a number of processes to enable you to work successfully in partnership with ASL
- raised your awareness about the value of an ASL contribution to the school environment
- demonstrated that the development of an ASL is an ongoing process.

Key Issues Raised in this Pack

- All ASL should:
  - work under the direction of a designated teacher(s)
  - be inducted into the school
  - carry out joint planning with a teacher
  - work alongside teachers until they are deemed to have the appropriate expertise, qualifications, disclosure certification, attitude and standards to work at distance.
- Stage One ASL should **never** be left unsupervised.
- Stage Two ASL may work at distance from a teacher, but schools are strongly recommended to take the following action before allowing them to do so:
  - Carry out a thorough risk assessment.
  - Ensure that an enhanced level disclosure certificate has been obtained.
  - Ensure that the ASL level of expertise, attitude towards pupils, class management and control, and application of the school's standards and policies are appropriate[1].
  - Agree a teaching programme.
  - Arrange to visit the ASL regularly to monitor their work.
- All adults working with children have a duty of care to ensure their health and safety.
- The welfare of the children is of paramount importance.
- ASL should feel comfortable and confident within the school.
- Monitoring and evaluation mechanisms should be in place.
- Appropriate development opportunities should be available to both ASL and teachers.

'**A very useful pack, offering clear advice, guidelines and routes forward for the ASL, and guidance for the teacher responsible.**'

Jane Powell, Chase High School

'**This resource provides comprehensive professional development for ASL supporting curriculum physical education.**'

Sue Wilkinson, Director, National College for Continuing Professional Development

---

1 For further information on recommended standards and competences, visit the afPE website (www.afpe.org.uk).

Summary

The Development of ASL

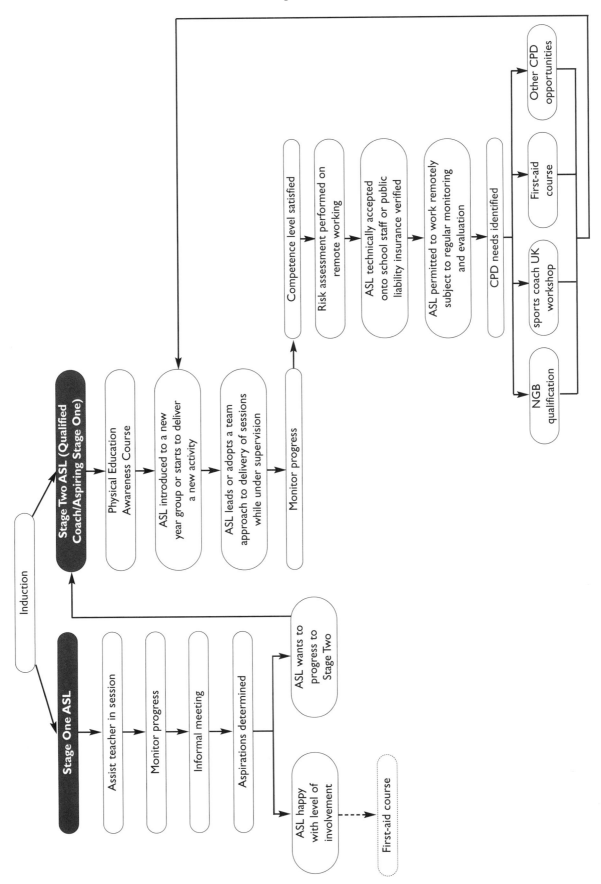

References

afPE (2006) *An Interpretation of the Workforce Remodelling Regulations and Guidance on Physical Education*. Available to download from the afPE members' website at www.afpe.org.uk

baalpe (2005) *Assessment for Learning in Physical Education*. Leeds: Coachwise Business Solutions. ISBN: 1-902523-79-2.

baalpe (2005) *Workforce Reform – Essential Safe Practice in Physical Education and School Sport*. Leeds: Coachwise Business Solutions.

baalpe (2006) *A Guide to Self-review in Physical Education*. Leeds: Coachwise Business Solutions. ISBN: 1-902523-98-9.

Crown (2003) *Every Child Matters Green Paper*.
To view this document, visit www.everychildmatters.gov.uk/publications

Crown (2005) *Workforce Reform and Professional Development*. To view this document, visit www.everychildmatters.gov.uk/deliveringservices/workforcereform

Physical Education Awareness Course for Adults Supporting Learning – To find out further information, please log on to www.afpe.org.uk or email helen.chadwick@afpe.org.uk

School Induction Pack
Adults Supporting Learning*
(Including Coaches and Volunteers)
A framework for development

Appendices

Disclosure Certification

Disclosure certification is one of a number of recommended pre-employment checks to assess adults' suitability to work with children. It is intended to contribute to an effective recruitment monitoring process for employers and voluntary organisations. Anyone appointed to work with young people, whether in a paid or voluntary capacity, may be asked by the employer to provide an enhanced disclosure certificate. This is a document containing information held by the police and relevant government departments, and is available from the Criminal Records Bureau (CRB).

The employer (LA/governors/trustees) will determine whether a certificate is needed. Schools are advised to check with their employer, if they are unsure whether an ASL needs to provide an enhanced disclosure certification.

ASL are responsible for applying for their own disclosure certificates. This can be done by:

- phoning the CRB on 0870-909 0844 and providing the details requested – the CRB inputs the details into the application form, prints it off and sends it to the applicant for signing and submission to a registered body (usually the employer)

or

- completing an application form provided by the employer.

ASL should submit their completed form to whoever originally requested it (eg school), along with any necessary originals of identity documents. The employer will countersign the form.

Note: Head teachers of LA schools cannot countersign on behalf of an LA.

If an individual has a number of jobs with different employers, for which disclosure certification is required, he/she may ask a new employer to accept sight of their first disclosure certificate, rather than applying for another one. Whether or not the employer will accept this will depend on:

- the level of certification
- how long ago it was awarded
- the nature of the position for which it was issued.

The information contained in disclosure certificates is confidential and is not passed on to schools by the employer. Schools will simply be informed whether or not any of the information indicates that the applicant may be unsuitable to work with children.

A criminal record does not automatically make someone unsuitable to work with young people. Suitability for employment should be judged in relation to:

- all pre-employment checks
- the nature of any offences
- the nature of the appointment
- the recency of the offence[1]
- the frequency of the offence
- the circumstances of the offence
- changes in the applicant's circumstances.

Certification will usually be logged by employers before destroying the disclosure certificate. All certificates must be destroyed after six months and employers must justify the need to retain certificates beyond this time.

---

1 Older offences may be less relevant than recent ones, but convictions for serious violence and sexual and substance abuse would continue to cause concern, regardless of when the offences took place.

Induction Checklist

Photocopy

Area of Induction	Has Seen	ASL Retained Copy	Signature of ASL (if applicable)	Date
Core Principles in Children's Sport				
Duty of Care				
Child Protection – *Safe and Sound*				
Code of Practice for Sports Coaches				
Welcome to the School				
Meeting the staff				
School staff handbook				
Policies				
School aims				
School rules				
Discipline and sanctions				
Behaviour				
Dress (ASL and pupil)				
Language and vocabulary (ASL and pupil)				
Equal opportunities				
Fair play				
Safeguarding and protecting children				
Procedures				
Health and safety policy				
Emergency contact details				
Accident and emergency procedures				
Supervision				
Disciplinary procedures and notice claims				
Payment arrangements (if applicable)				
Self-declaration form/CRB enhanced level disclosure				
NGB qualification validity				
Appropriate insurance cover (see footnote 1 on page 4)				
Safeguarding and protecting children training[1]				
Agreement to NGB/sports coach UK code of practice				
Up-to-date first-aid qualifications				

Please photocopy for each ASL involved. Both the ASL and the school will keep a copy.

1 Direct delivery within last 2–3 years – see CPSU website for 'recognised' courses/workshops – www.thecpsu.org.uk

Sample Session Plan

Date of session:		Venue:

Time:	Duration:	Number of young people:

Name of group:

Equipment needed:

Teaching outcomes:	Learning outcomes:
•	•
•	•
•	•

	Time
Warm-up/introduction:	
Main content:	
Cool-down/summary:	
Evaluation of session:	

Injuries/incidents:	Feedback/action to be taken:

Sample Delivery Log

photocopy

Date		Time		Venue	
Class teacher					
Number of young people	School year	1	2	3	4	5	6	7	8	9	10	11	12	13
Title of session/ activity					
Learning outcomes					
My involvement:					

Sample Feedback and Evaluation Forms   Photocopy

Young People's Questionnaire

What did you think of the sessions?

Answer each of the following by ticking **one** box after each statement.

	Yes	Don't know	No
I The sessions were great fun.			
2 I learned a lot of new skills.			
3 I was always involved.			
4 I was never bored.			
5 There was plenty of equipment for use.			
6 Now, list the new activities you would like to try:			

_____

_____

_____

_____

_____

_____

_____

These statements may need to be explained and read aloud to participants, depending on their age and stage of development.

Sample Feedback and Evaluation Forms *Photocopy*

ASL Feedback

Read each statement and circle **one** letter that you deem to be most appropriate to that statement.

Key: A Agree strongly
    B Agree
    C Neutral
    D Disagree
    E Disagree strongly

Add further statements to the list if required.

	Statements	Circle one letter	Comments/changes required
1	My role as a coach/helper has been clearly explained to me.	A B C D E	_____
2	The sessions are well organised.	A B C D E	_____
3	Sufficient equipment and resources are supplied.	A B C D E	_____
4	The facilities are suitable and in good order.	A B C D E	_____
5	I am valued for the job I do.	A B C D E	_____
6	I am working as part of a team.	A B C D E	_____
7	The teacher is open to suggestions/comments.	A B C D E	_____
8	I have been offered CPD opportunities to further my qualifications.	A B C D E	_____
9	I have been advised on child protection issues and where to get further information.	A B C D E	_____
10	The young people really enjoy the sessions.	A B C D E	_____
11	I have learned a lot from my involvement in this process.	A B C D E	_____
12	I would be delighted to continue working in this school.	A B C D E	_____
13	_____	A B C D E	_____
14	_____	A B C D E	_____

Sample Feedback and Evaluation Forms

Photocopy

Evaluation of Sessions

This form can be used to provide feedback to ASL after assisting or leading the delivery of a session. This information can be stored in a development portfolio and, over time, can be used to document progression and development.

Name of evaluator _____

Date of evaluation _____

Name of ASL _____

Type of session _____

What went well?	What could have gone better?	Changes required

Training Organisations and Further Contacts

National Governing Bodies of Sport

Links to NGB websites are available on the Sport England and Central Council of Physical Recreation (CCPR) websites (see below for the relevant website addresses).

afPE
Worcester Office
University College Worcester
Henwick Grove
Worcester WR2 6AJ
Tel: 01905-855 584
Email: simon.leach@afpe.org.uk
Website: www.afpe.org.uk

afPE
Building 25
London Road
Reading RG1 5AQ

British Red Cross (BRC)
UK Office
44 Moorfields
London EC2Y 9AL
Tel: 0870-170 7000
Fax: 020-7562 2000
Email: information@redcross.org.uk
Website: www.redcross.org.uk

Central Council of Physical Recreation (CCPR)
Francis House
Francis Street
London SW1P 1DE
Tel: 020-7854 8500
Fax: 020-7854 8501
Email: info@ccpr.org.uk
Website: www.ccpr.org.uk

Child Protection in Sport Unit
NSPCC National Training Centre
3 Gilmour Close
Beaumont Leys
Leicester LE4 1EZ
Tel: 0116-234 7278/7217
Fax: 0116-234 7251
Email: cpsu@nspcc.org.uk
Website: www.thecpsu.org.uk

Sport England
3rd Floor Victoria House
Bloomsbury Square
London WC1B 4SE
Tel: 08458-508 508
Fax: 020-7383 5740
Email: info@sportengland.org
Website: www.sportengland.org

sports coach UK
114 Cardigan Road
Headingley
Leeds LS6 3BJ
Tel: 0113-274 4802
Fax: 0113-275 5019
Email: coaching@sportscoachuk.org
Website: www.sportscoachuk.org

Sports Leaders UK
23–25 Linford Forum
Rockingham Drive
Linford Wood
Milton Keynes MK14 6LY
Tel: 01908-689 180
Fax: 01908-393 744
Email: info@sportsleaders.org
Website: www.bst.org.uk

Youth Sport Trust (YST)
Sir John Beckwith Centre for Sport
Loughborough University
Loughborough
Leicestershire LE11 3TU
Tel: 01509-226 600
Fax: 01509-210 851
Email: info@youthsporttrust.org
Website: www.youthsporttrust.org

Safe and Sound Leaflet

What signs might register concern?

Coaches have a moral and even legal responsibility to support and care for young people/disabled adults, not only while they are on the club premises but also if they suspect abuse is taking place elsewhere.

There are physical and behavioural signs that might raise your concern about the welfare or safety of a performer. Some examples include:

- unexplained bruising or injuries and reluctance to talk about them
- unexplained changes in behaviour – becoming aggressive, withdrawn or unhappy
- something said by a performer or a peer, who may identify a coach as a trusted person with whom to share concerns
- a change observed over a long period of time (eg the person losing weight or becoming increasingly dirty or unkempt)
- sexually explicit behaviour and language.

These signs are indicators, not confirmation of abuse. However, if you notice any of these signs regularly or more than one sign, you should record and report your concerns.

Abuse may result from various causes through the misuse of power by adults or peers:

- **Neglect** (eg lack of food, warmth, supervision, attention, love and affection). In sport, this may result from a failure to ensure performers are safe, free from risk of excessive cold, heat, or injury.

- **Physical abuse** (eg hitting, shaking, squeezing, biting, burning). In sport, this may result if the nature or intensity of training is inappropriate for the capacity of the performer; or where drugs or alcohol (specifically with U18s) are advocated or tolerated.

- **Sexual abuse** (eg any form of sexual behaviour between an adult and a young person, or use of pornographic material). In sport, this may be the result of coaches or older performers involving young/disabled performers in any form of sexual activity (eg sexual language, touching or relationships).

- **Emotional abuse** (eg wherever there is any other form of abuse as well as the withholding of love or affection, overprotection, frequent use of shouting or taunts). In sport, this may occur if performers are subject to constant criticism, bullying (by coach, parents or peers), taunting or unrealistic pressure to perform to high expectations.

- **Bullying** In some cases the abuser may be a young person rather than an adult. Bullying may be seen as deliberately hurtful behaviour, usually repeated over a period of time, where it is difficult for those bullied to defend themselves. It can take many forms including physical (eg hitting, kicking or theft), verbal (eg racist or homophobic remarks, threats or name calling) and emotional (eg isolation from the activities and social acceptance of the peer group).

In some cases it is hard to distinguish between poor coaching practice and abuse. Your responsibility is to do everything within your power to ensure your coaching practice is beyond reproach.

Acceptable practice, poor practice or abuse?

Is it okay to push young performers so hard that they are physically sick? This may be deemed acceptable if it occurs occasionally when coaching elite performers. However, it may constitute poor practice and even abuse, if it occurs frequently and/or is accompanied by distress.

Safe and Sound Leaflet

Do you know what to do if a child is distressed by another person's behaviour?

If you are worried, remember it is not your responsibility to decide if abuse is taking place but it is your responsibility to act on your concerns and do something about it.

Can you promise not to tell anyone?

If you suspect a child is being abused, you will have to report your concerns in order that the abuse is investigated and stopped. Never make promises you cannot keep.

If a performer tells you about someone's behaviour (eg an adult or another young person) which he/she finds disturbing, always:

- stay calm and reassure the person – ensure he/she is safe, feels safe and does not feel to blame for what has happened

- listen carefully, show and tell the performer that you are taking seriously what is being said

- be honest, explain you will have to tell someone else to help stop the behaviour that is distressing

- make a note of what was said as soon as possible after the event

- maintain confidentiality – only share the information on a need to know basis and if it will help the performer

- gain medical attention immediately if required and if appropriate, contact the police or social services.

Safe and Sound Leaflet

It is never too late to ask for help.

If you were abused in the past, you can still seek help to deal with how you feel. There are many confidential helplines and organisations in the phonebook. Please find the courage to call – especially if the perpetrator is still involved in sport and has access to other young vulnerable people.

Do you know what to do if you are concerned about someone's behaviour?

It is your responsibility to act if you are concerned about the behaviour of an adult towards a performer or if you feel a young person/disabled adult is being bullied:

- Always follow your organisation's child protection guidelines.
- Report your concerns with full details to the senior person in charge (or someone you can trust) – it is then the responsibility of that person in charge to act.
- If the person in charge is not available, the concerns are about him/her, or you do not feel appropriate action has been taken, you must contact the social services or the police. Both organisations have specialist units trained to deal with these situations and their numbers are in the phone book.

Should you report your concerns straight away?

If you are concerned about the welfare or safety of a performer, you must report your concerns to a senior person or an expert. If you are unsure what to do or need reassurance, seek advice from the NSPCC (0800-800 5000), ChildLine (0800-1111), the police or social services.

How can you protect yourself?

To prevent the possibility of allegations about your coaching, adopt the good practice guidelines advocated by your governing body and the advice in this leaflet. In addition to the points made earlier, remember to follow the advice below:

- Always work in an open environment – avoid private locations (eg taking performers to your home).
- Maintain a safe and appropriate distance with performers (eg it is not appropriate to have an intimate relationship with a young performer or to share a room with him/her).
- Involve parents and/or guardians wherever possible.
- Be aware of your organisation's child protection policy and your responsibilities.
- Sign up and adhere to a coach's code of practice (club, governing body or sports coach UK).
- Avoid any horseplay, sexually suggestive comments or language.
- Gain further child protection information, awareness and knowledge (see resources and workshops section).

Should you drive him/her home?

Remember, if there is no other viable option, it is okay for a coach to give one young person a lift in the car, but it is important to inform the parents. This may be acceptable as a one-off but it is very unwise to do this regularly or frequently.

Safe and Sound Leaflet

Do you have any other concerns?

Is your coaching practice safe and sound? Is your practice beyond reproach? Can you answer all the questions on this leaflet?

This appendix contains some of the steps for safe and sound sport for all. sports coach UK provides up-to-date information and workshops to supply more comprehensive advice and training:

- **Workshops:** *Safeguarding and Protecting Children, The Responsible Sports Coach, Coaching and the Law, Analysing your Coaching, Coaching Methods and Communication, Coaching Disabled Performers, Understanding Eating Disorders.*

- **Resources:** *Safeguarding and Protecting Children, Code of Practice for Sports Coaches* (leaflet), *Making Sport Fun* (booklet), *The Successful Coach* (handbook), *How to Coach Children in Sport* (booklet), *Coaching Young Performers* (handbook).

NB Some of the above resources are complimentary with their corresponding sports coach UK workshop.

Contact sports coach UK for further details:

sports coach UK
114 Cardigan Road
Headingley
Leeds LS6 3BJ
Tel: 0113-274 4802
Fax: 0113-275 5019
Email: coaching@sportscoachuk.org
Website: www.sportscoachuk.org

The information in this appendix is taken from sports coach UK's *Safe and Sound* leaflet. No part of it may be reproduced in any format without the prior written permission of the copyright holder.

Copies of the *Safe and Sound* leaflet can be purchased from:	All copyright enquiries should be addressed to :
Coachwise 1st4sport Coachwise Ltd Chelsea Close Off Amberley Road Armley Leeds LS12 4HP Tel: 0113-201 5555 Fax: 0113-231 9606 Email: enquiries@1st4sport.com Website: www.1st4sport.com	**Coachwise Business Solutions** Coachwise Ltd Chelsea Close Off Amberley Road Armley Leeds LS12 4HP Tel: 0113-231 1310 Fax: 0113-231 9606 Email: enquiries@coachwisesolutions.co.uk Website: www.coachwisesolutions.co.uk

Great Coaches ... Great Sport

SPORT ENGLAND

© The National Coaching Foundation and The NSPCC, 2005

Photographs courtesy of www.actionplus.co.uk, Supersport and Karen Fuches

Rights

Relationships

Responsibilities

for Sports Coaches

Code of Practice

Coaches play a crucial role in the development of any sport and in the lives of the athletes they coach. Good coaches ensure that individuals in sport have positive experiences and are therefore more likely to continue in their sport and achieve their potential.

Coaching, as an emerging profession, must demonstrate at all levels a high degree of honesty, integrity and competence. The need for coaches to understand and act on their responsibilities is of critical importance to sport, as is the need to protect the key concept of participation for fun and enjoyment as well as achievement. This is implicit within good coaching practice and promotes a professional image of the good practitioner. This code of conduct defines all that is best in good coaching practice.

- **Rights**

  Coaches must respect and champion the rights of every individual to participate in sport.

- **Relationships**

  Coaches must develop a relationship with athletes (and others) based on openness, honesty, mutual trust and respect.

- **Responsibilities – personal standards**

  Coaches must demonstrate proper personal behaviour and conduct at all times.

- **Responsibilities – professional standards**

  To maximise benefits and minimise the risks to athletes, coaches must attain a high level of competence through qualifications and a commitment to ongoing training that ensures safe and correct practice.

Great Coaches ... Great Sport

Code of Practice for Sports Coaches

Principle	Statement	Issues	Actions
Rights	Coaches must respect and champion the rights of every individual to participate in sport	Coaches should: • assist in the creation of an environment where every individual has the opportunity to participate in a sport or activity of their choice • create and maintain an environment free of fear and harassment • recognise the rights of all athletes to be treated as individuals • recognise the rights of athletes to confer with other coaches and experts • promote the concept of a balanced lifestyle, supporting the well-being of the athlete both in and out of the sport.	• Treat all individuals in sport with respect at all times. • Do not discriminate on the grounds of gender, marital status, race, colour, disability, sexuality, age, occupation, religion or political opinion. • Do not condone or allow to go unchallenged any form of discrimination. • Do not publicly criticise or engage in demeaning descriptions of others. • Be discreet in any conversations about athletes, coaches or any other individuals. • Communicate with and provide feedback to athletes in a manner which reflects respect and care.

Code of Practice for Sports Coaches

Principle	Statement	Issues	Actions
Relationships	Coaches must develop a relationship with athletes (and others) based on openness, honesty, mutual trust and respect	Coaches: • must not engage in behaviour that constitutes any form of abuse (physical, sexual, emotional, neglect, bullying)	• Be aware of the physical needs of athletes, especially those still growing, and ensure that training loads and intensities are appropriate. • Ensure that physical contact is appropriate and necessary and is carried out within recommended guidelines with the athlete's full consent and approval. • Do not engage in any form of sexually related contact with an under age athlete. This is strictly forbidden as is sexual innuendo, flirting or inappropriate gestures and terms.
		• should promote the welfare and best interests of their athletes • must avoid sexual intimacy with athletes either while coaching them or in the period of time immediately following the end of the coaching relationship	• Inform parents or guardians immediately if you are at all concerned about the welfare of a child. • Discuss with parents and other interested parties the potential impact of the programme on the athlete. • Arrange to transfer an athlete to another coach if it is clear that an intimate relationship is developing.
		• must take action if they have a concern about the behaviour of an adult towards a child	• Know and understand the relevant NGB or employer policies and procedures in this regard. • Follow the reporting procedures laid down by your NGB or employer if you have a concern – non-action is unacceptable.
		• should empower athletes to be responsible for their own decisions	• Respect athletes' opinions when making decisions about their participation in their sport. • Encourage athletes to take responsibility for their own development and actions. • Allow athletes to discuss and participate in the decision-making process.
		• should clarify the nature of the coaching services being offered to athletes	• Discuss and agree with athletes what information is confidential. • Inform athletes or their parents of the requirements of the sport. • Inform athletes or their parents of any potential costs involved in accessing the coaching services on offer.
		• should communicate and cooperate with other organisations and individuals in the best interests of athletes.	• Be aware of and communicate on any conflict of interest as soon as it becomes apparent. • Do not work with any other coach's athlete without first discussing or agreeing it with both the coach and the athlete involved. • Identify and agree with athletes which other experts or organisations could offer appropriate services.

Relationships

Code of Practice for Sports Coaches

Principle	Statement	Issues	Actions
Responsibilites – personal standards	Coaches must demonstrate proper personal behaviour and conduct at all times	Coaches: • must be fair, honest and considerate to athletes and others in their sport • should project an image of health, cleanliness and functional efficiency • must be positive role models for athletes at all times.	• Operate within the rules and the spirit of your sport. • Educate athletes on issues relating to the use of performance-enhancing drugs in sport and cooperate fully with UK Sport and NGB policies. • Maintain the same level of interest and support when an athlete is sick or injured. • Display high standards in use of language, manner, punctuality, preparation and presentation. • Encourage athletes to display the same qualities. • Do not smoke, drink alcohol or use recreational drugs before or while coaching. This reflects a negative image and could compromise the safety of your athletes. • Display control, respect, dignity and professionalism to all involved in your sport.

Code of Practice for Sports Coaches

Principle	Statement	Issues	Actions
Responsibilites – professional standards	To maximise benefits and minimise the risks to athletes, coaches must attain a high level of competence through qualifications and a commitment to ongoing training that ensures safe and correct practice	Coaches will: • ensure that the environment is as safe as possible, taking into account and minimising possible risks • promote the execution of safe and correct practice • be professional and accept responsibility for their actions • make a commitment to providing a quality service to their athletes • actively promote the positive benefits to society of participation in sport • contribute to the development of coaching as a profession by exchanging knowledge and ideas with others • gain NGB coaching qualifications appropriate to the level at which they coach.	• Follow the guidelines of your NGB or employer. • Plan all sessions so they meet the needs of the athletes and are progressive and appropriate. • Maintain appropriate records of your athletes. • Recognise and accept when it is appropriate to refer an athlete to another coach or specialist. • Seek to achieve the highest level of qualification available. • Attend Continuing Professional Development (CPD) to maintain up-to-date knowledge of technical developments in your sport. • Attend CPD to maintain up-to-date knowledge and understanding of other issues that might impact on both you and your athletes. • Be aware of the social issues and how your sport can contribute to local, regional or national initiatives. • Actively participate in recruitment and education opportunities in your sport. • Actively contribute to local, regional and national initiatives to improve the standards and quality of coaching both in your sport and sport in general. • Practise in an open and transparent fashion that encourages other coaches to contribute to or learn from your knowledge and experience. • Engage in self-analysis and reflection to identify your professional needs. • Seek continuous professional development opportunities to develop your coaching skills and update your knowledge. • Manage your lifestyle and coaching commitments to avoid burnout that might impair your performance. • Do not assume responsibility for any role for which you are not qualified or prepared. • Do not misrepresent your level of qualification.

Responsibilities – professional standards

Code of Practice for Sports Coaches

Implementation Issues

It is recognised and identified by the Ethics Review Group that a code of practice in isolation is of minimal value. In order for this code to fully impact on coaching practice and behaviour, it must:

- be incorporated into NGB or employer constitutions and governance documents

- be a constituent part of a policy and procedure for dealing with allegations and complaints

- be used as the definitive guide and benchmark measure of coaching practice in determining any need for sanctions against a coach

- be fully incorporated into coach education processes

- be assessed as part of the coach accreditation process

- be supported by the appropriate training and resources.

sports coach UK has developed a suite of training resources that underpin many of the concepts contained within this Code of Practice for Sports Coaches. These are:

- Safeguarding and Protecting Children

- Equity in Your Coaching

- The Responsible Sports Coach

- Coaching and the Law

sports coach UK will use this code of practice as a measure of coaching practice to determine the suitability of coaches retaining access to the sports coach UK membership benefits. sports coach UK will support a national governing body in implementing this code of practice by assisting in developing appropriate policies and procedures for dealing with allegations and complaints based on coaching practice. Criminal allegations will be dealt with by the appropriate authority and may impact on access to sports coach UK benefits.

The information in this appendix is taken from sports coach UK's *Code of Practice for Sports Coaches,* which can be purchased from Coachwise 1st4sport. No part of it may be reproduced in any format without the prior written permission of the copyright holder.

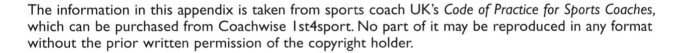

Copies of the *Code of Practice for Sports Coaches* leaflet can be purchased from:

Coachwise 1st4sport
Coachwise Ltd
Chelsea Close
Off Amberley Road
Armley
Leeds LS12 4HP
Tel: 0113-201 5555
Fax: 0113-231 9606
Email: enquiries@1st4sport.com
Website: www.1st4sport.com

All copyright enquiries should be addressed to :

Coachwise Business Solutions
Coachwise Ltd
Chelsea Close
Off Amberley Road
Armley
Leeds LS12 4HP
Tel: 0113-231 1310
Fax: 0113-231 9606
Email: enquiries@coachwisesolutions.co.uk
Website: www.coachwisesolutions.co.uk

© The National Coaching Fondration, 2005

Photographs courtesy of sports coach UK